I0756627

ASTRONOMICAL WEATHER

JOHN SHERIDAN THOMAS

authorHOUSE

AuthorHouse™
1663 Liberty Drive
Bloomington, IN 47403
www.authorhouse.com
Phone: 833-262-8899

Published by AuthorHouse 09/02/2020

ISBN: 978-1-7283-7115-3 (sc)
ISBN: 978-1-7283-7114-6 (e)

Print information available on the last page.

CONTENTS

FOREWORD

Not long ago, one who publically displayed disbelief that carbon dioxide causes global warming would get labeled as a climate denier; implying Neanderthal or worse. Thus doubters tended to stay quiet, biding their time, perhaps hoping for a global freeze to exonerate them.

Then something changed in the climate atmosphere; maybe it was posturing of liberal political activists claiming global warming Armageddon is just 10 years out. This seems way over-the-top, perhaps exposing the climate threat as mostly hype aimed at intimidating us, the electorate.

In 2006 Al Gore in "An inconvenient Truth" claimed the deadline to cease carbon consumption was just 10 years out. Then in 2007 he wrote: "I predict the ice caps will melt by 2014."

Apparently some politicians believe our collective memory has a limit of 10 years. Or perhaps more likely, they believe their political horizons do not reach beyond a decade.

At the heart of our nation's wealth is democracy and free enterprise. Curtailing carbon-based energy without a competitive alternative is sure to produce an economic disaster.

Climate Science aka Climatology focuses on the structure and dynamics of earth's behavior; and the causes and consequences of long term change, especially global warming. It aims to identify long range climate trends rather than seasonal or other short term weather variations that occur throughout the year.

This science involves the dynamics of molecules of hydrogen, oxygen and carbon in earth's atmosphere. Yet practitioners have not inquired deeply into characteristics of the solar system or the vast universe beyond as to their influence on earth's ecosystem.

I sifted through dozens of internet sources concerned with global warming; and looked closely at the earth's environment as driven predominantly by the solar system; especially the sun's impact on earthly climate.

Perhaps the most stunning finding of this enquiry was that this "climate science" supporting global warming does not recognize any celestial influence on earth's climate beyond the contemporary impact of the sun. Moreover, there are two other critical fields of enquiry, astronomy and astrophysics, which seem to have been bypassed in the framing of the global climate issue.

1

INTRODUCTION

Before Christ, some eight centuries before, the world was flat; that was the prevailing wisdom. The ends of the world must be out there somewhere; or perhaps not. Planet earth is flat to the eye and rides on air like the sun; or maybe it is just a disk floating in an infinite ocean.

In 1492 Christopher Columbus set out to Asia, choosing to sail west rather than hiking overland eastward as Marco

Polo had done in 1275. Columbus knew the earth was round, and set out to prove it. He spent 3½ years getting to Shang-Tu, the capital of Kublai Khan. Surprisingly (to Columbus) the American continents were in his way; thus he accidentally discovered America.

Twenty-seven years later (1519) Ferdinand Magellan, with an armada of five ships and 260 men, sailed westward across the Atlantic through the Strait of Magellan into the Pacific Ocean, then the Indian Ocean. Magellan and many crewmen died during this trek, but one ship and 18 men completed the world circle in the year 1522. Poof, the flat earth became round!

Prior to the 20th century we had neither the means nor the desire to dissect weather variations; there was no thought that human activity might affect climate. When scholars thought beyond earth, it was about the moon, the sun, and beyond.

Entering the 20th century and the industrial revolution; we produced the internal combustion engine. Concurrently we discovered many other uses for carbon-based energy to the great benefit of mankind, albeit unevenly around the globe.

More recently, just a half century ago, there were several "mysterious" airplane accidents, including three passenger planes disappearing off the coast of Florida in an area known as the Bermuda Triangle. Over time, accidents in the Bermuda triangle led to the lore that an evil power was causing them. Alas, that evil power was never found; it just faded away.

Humanity has become dependent on fossil fuels for heating and cooling, for transportation, and to support our military-industrial complex. Without carbon-based energy we could not fly around the world or anywhere in between.

Our great economic progress is threatened by efforts to curtail fossil fuels for fear that planet earth otherwise will overheat.

It was observed that trace amounts of CO_2 in the atmosphere from burning oil, gasoline and coal were increasing. Scientists realized that CO_2 in the lower atmosphere tended to reflect heat radiating from earth.

This reflection, many believe, changes the balance of heat flowing from the sun to earth and back into space, inexorably raising earth's temperature. Thus the notion of global warming was borne and a climate science to explain it.

The proposed solution, abandoning carbon fuels, poses an economic threat to modern civilization. Eliminating fossil fuels would have massive negative economic consequences to most of the world's population.

II

WARMING EARTH

We have been burning oil, gas, and coal in increasing amounts over the past 150 years, a period that coincides roughly with the industrial revolution. Most of the world depends on fossil fuels; so much so that it is difficult to imagine life without them.

Now we face the possibility that carbon-based fuels will be our undoing. The greatest fear, climate scientists say, is earth will warm and polar ice will melt, causing massive flooding of the world's low-lying cities.

About a decade ago, the National Geographic displayed on its front cover the Statue of Liberty submerged in some 50 feet of rising waters. This article warned us that world-wide flooding was coming if we continued burning fossil fuels.

Earthly Temperatures

To evaluate this threat we must critically examine the theory. The first step is to determine and track earth's temperatures, past and present; a daunting task.

Earth's circumference is 25,000 miles, and the total plane surface area (discounting a multitude of mountains and valleys throughout the planet) is roughly 197 million square miles (according to Google). Venus is slightly smaller at 178 million square miles.

It is generally recognized that global temperatures have increased modestly throughout the last century, less than one degree centigrade over 120 years.

However it is notable that there was little increase from 1940 through 1970; and for the 40-year period from 1880 to 1920.

The temperature changes as you rise higher into the troposphere. Figure 1 below shows the temperature trend in the lower troposphere measured by satellite-mounted microwave sounding units.

FIGURE 1: Troposphere Temperatures

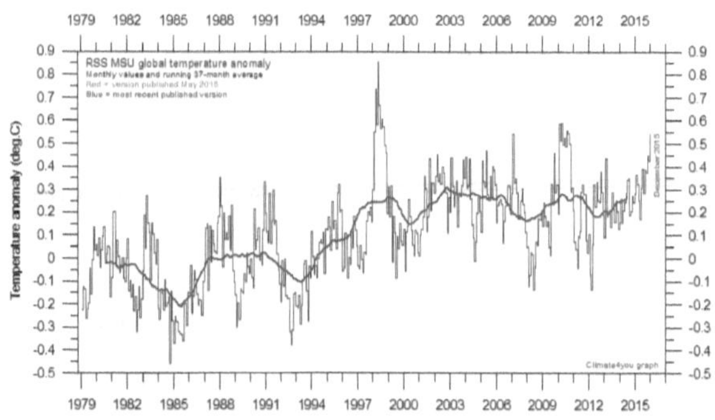

This chart was published on the web site Climate4you. Here we see in the lower troposphere (that is earth's atmosphere from ground up to about 50 km) temperatures were nearly flat from 1980 through 1994; then for the next eight years they rose steadily. Then notable there was no increase from 2002 to 2016.

Cooling World?

With all of the attention on warming, it is surprising that earth was actually cooling not long ago. In 1975 Newsweek published an article titled "The Cooling World". According to Newsweek, this cooling would lead to a drastic decline in food production.

Meteorologists thought this cooling would reduce agricultural productivity for the rest of the century. Not to be outdone, Time Magazine published a featured article "Another Ice Age" painting this bleak picture of a cooling earth:

"When meteorologists measure temperatures around the globe, they find the atmosphere has been growing gradually cooler for the past three decades. The trend shows no indication of reversing."

This is puzzling; a mini ice age in the middle of global warming; earthly chilling in the midst of the world's great carbon-fueled economic expansion. Then as this chill ran its course, earth resumed warming. Observers promptly reconnected the dots between increasing CO_2 and rising global temperatures.

Why Warming?

CO_2 in the lower atmosphere has a tendency to reflect heat radiating up from earth. This reflection increases the balance of heat retained by earth.

One might have thought "Good, we are saved from a coming ice age." Contrarily, the notion took hold that carbon-induced global warming is the real threat. This latter-day warming will melt polar ice; oceans will rise; continents will flood.

Catastrophic warming and flooding have become the focus along with a science to support this theory. It is an "existential" threat. (An over-used adjective in today's vernacular!)

Warming Pattern

Past temperature patterns do not correlate well with a steady rise of atmospheric CO_2. The warming theory tells us when atmospheric carbon increases, temperatures increase; and these increases are proportional and concurrent. Oddly the lower troposphere doesn't behave; it displays no consistency in temperatures compared to carbon dioxide.

Plentiful Excuses

For the past 40 years records show inconsistencies between global temperatures and temperatures projected by the carbon-warming theory. Excuses for this lack of correlation between CO_2 and temperature are plentiful. Here are three.

1. **These temperature fluctuations are statistically insignificant.**
2. **Warming was offset by reduced solar irradiance during a period of low sunspot activity.**
3. **The persistence on the negative phase of the winter of 2009/10 was characterized by record North-Atlantic Oscillation.**

Solar irradiance and North-Atlantic Oscillation! So, climate does not depend on CO_2 alone. Needing to explain further, NASA hedges with these statements:

**"It is still a pretty good approximation
to say that the whole is the sum of the**

parts, but as we get into more details, the non-linearity looms large.

That means we need to be more careful in judging the importance of different drivers in climate change."

Fits and Starts

Patrick Michaels, climatologist for the Cato Institute, reported global temperatures have moved in fits and starts since the Little Ice Age. Further, he says, these movements are unrelated to CO_2 and otherwise unexplained. Temperatures have been going up modestly in fits and starts since before the first automobile was invented. Here is his description of global temperatures over the past 150 years.

> "Surface temperatures are indeed increasing slightly. They've being going up in fits and starts for more than 150 years . . . since a pestilent period known as the Little Ice Age. Even in the 20th century, unexplained temperature variances continued. Before CO_2 emissions could have warmed us much, temperatures rose ¾ of a degree between 1910 and World War II. They then cooled down a bit, only to warm again from the mid1970's to the late '90s."

Temperature variations before the 20th century are indeed inconvenient facts as they contradict the warming theory.

Not only are climate "experts" unable to explain temperatures of centuries ago, they cannot explain most variations of the last 100 years. Alas, climate does not behave the way the theory says it should.

Nevertheless, while they cannot explain the past, they eagerly predict the future!

Do We Really Know?

Recording global temperatures is a daunting challenge. Readings are taken unevenly around the globe; then weighted to produce a global balance. Does this adjustment process produce accurate results upon which to place massive economic constraints on civilization? Alternatively, we might wonder: are those manipulating the climate data really objective?

Recycling H_2O

Of course water evaporates faster in warm weather than in cold; so as earth warms, evaporation accelerates. This evaporation and the resulting clouds lower temperatures. Dr. Clive Best, Physicist, confirms this process:

"The natural cyclical change in global cloud-cover has a greater impact

on global temperatures that CO_2. The gradual reduction in net cloud cover explains over 50% of global warming observed during the 1080's and 1990's; and the hiatus in warming since 1998 coincides with stabilization of cloud forcing."

There is no doubt that evaporation then cloud formation increase as earth warms. The obvious consequence is that the relationship between airborne CO_2 and warming is not linear.

Increases in CO_2 will have decreasing impact on global temperatures.

Confirming this non-linearity, NASA conceded there are multiple drivers of climate change.

III

CARBON FACTOR

Atmospheric CO_2 increased steadily over the last century as carbon fuels grew into major energy sources. We invented the internal combustion engine and built entirely new industries reliant upon carbon-based fuels: coal, oil and natural gas.

Carbon Dioxide – The Means

Presumably earth warms proportional to the increase in airborne CO_2; as we burn carbon fuels – coal, oil and gas – earth's mean temperature goes up. We all have seen the graphs of increasing atmospheric CO_2 over the past century.

Presently atmospheric CO_2 is approximately 400 parts per million, having roughly doubled over the past 150 to 200 years throughout the rapidly growing industrial age. Automobiles, coal-fired railroad trains, and air travel increased the atmospheric CO_2 from trace amounts, climbing steadily upward; now accounting for 400 parts per million.

Four hundred parts per million sounds like a lot of carbon dioxide. But when it is expressed as a decimal, it equals 0.000400 parts. This tiny bit is threatening our earthly existence!

Flooding – The Result

The global flooding derives from the belief that the Greenland ice sheet would melt as earth warms.

This ice sheet is so large that, according to analysts, a melt-down would cause oceans to rise some 25 feet.

As we burn carbon fuels, earth will inexorably warm. Seas will rise as temperatures go up, abetted by melting polar ice caps. These rising waters will inundate low-lying coastal lands, and flood major population centers. Like ancient Atlantis, Miami will disappear under the sea. Massive disruptions will occur.

They say global warming is occurring. If no mitigating actions are taken, disruptions in the earth's physical and ecological systems, social systems, security and human health are likely to occur.

The theory holds that the relationship between CO_2 emissions and global temperature is **direct and linear**; incremental increases in airborne CO_2 have the same warming impact at 70 degrees as at say 75 degrees. There is no diminishing impact; no saturation; nor are there any celestial events that may affect these earthly temperatures. This is what we are told.

Global Model

Schematically the formula for the carbon-driven global warming theory is:

$$T = c + f\,(CO_2)$$

In this formula T is the global average temperature; c and f are constants; and CO_2 is airborne carbon dioxide. One must wonder how the solar system could be so simple.

Surely increasing atmospheric CO_2 has a warming dimension; yet temperatures have risen and fallen sporadically over last 150 years while we steadily consumed more and more oil, coal and gas.

There is no explanation for periods contrary to an expected steady warming; nor is there an explanation for global climate variations over prior centuries before Henry Ford built the "Tin Lizzy".

The correlation between CO_2 and global temperature is claimed to be linear: temperature increases will be directly proportional to CO_2. This linearity supposedly applies over a range of CO_2 from 100 to at least 500 ppm (parts per million).

Professor Happer (Princeton) disputes this linear CO_2 warming formula. He writes: "At 400 ppm we are well into the saturation region." His formula shows Doubling CO_2 to 800 ppm raises the temperature by 1^0 C. He advised me:

"To get 2^0 C of warming you have to quadruple the CO_2 concentration to 1600 ppm."

Air Pollution

Burning fossil fuels emits various chemical compounds and solid particles. The EPA identifies five of them as air pollutants. They are ozone, solid particles, carbon monoxide, sulfur dioxide, nitrogen dioxide. Carbon dioxide is not one of them!

The CO_2 Problem

Humans cause most carbon dioxide emissions; and these emissions are blamed for earth's temperature increases.

There is a basic deficiency with that notion. When applied retroactively, the formula produces temperature estimates that quite often are at substantial variance from the actual recorded temperatures for most of the 20th century, the period from which the entire warming theory was conceived.

There is the hardly noticed fact about carbon dioxide emissions that strongly suggests a non-linear relationship between CO_2 and world temperatures. Every year a considerable proportion of airborne CO_2 returns to earth; the increase in CO_2 retained in the atmosphere is less than one-half the annual emissions.

Recorded data is so tenuous it is impossible to determine whether it is linear or not. It is **highly likely** that CO_2 increments have declining impact on temperatures as they increase. Meanwhile other unrecognized climate factors continue to muddy expectations.

Presently the annual increase in retained CO_2 is about one-third of the amount emitted. This retained portion is declining; requiring more and more emissions to achieve incremental increases in retained CO_2. This is due at least in part to increasing cloud formation and rainfall which reduce surface temperatures.

IV

RISING SEAS

Suppose the ocean surface temperature continues to warm over the next 130 years by the same amount as the past 130 years - about one degree Fahrenheit. This warming would cause oceans to rise 3 to 4 inches by thermal expansion. (As air temperature warms, oceans warm from the top down to the thermocline – roughly 400 to 800 meters below the ocean surface.)

Thermal expansion of the oceans is not a substantial threat. That leaves only the threat of Greenland's ice sheet melting. (It is not clear why there was no equal claim for the South Pole.) Supposedly the Greenland meltdown would cause the seas to rise 25 feet. This threat was published in the National geographic, September 2013.

The National Geographic claimed 136 large coastal cities are at risk from sea-level rise. One-third of this rising sea water comes from thermal expansion.

The rest, they say, would come from melting of land ice – specifically the Greenland ice sheet. This is a false threat (See Chapter IX - Greenland Scam).

Melting Ice and Snow

According to the flooding manifesto, most of the water raising sea levels will come from melting the polar ice cap; the physics is a bit subtle. When **floating** ice melts, the water level does not rise; because melting ice contracts. As to snow: tightly packed snow has a density roughly of ½ that of water; when it melts, it contracts some 50%, or nearly 90% for dry snowflakes. These characteristics substantially discount the Greenland melting – world flooding threat.

Hurricane Sandy

A late-season tropical storm Sandy swept through the Caribbean and up the East coast in late October 2012. This storm, hurricane Sandy, left dozens dead, thousands homeless and millions without power. Deaths included 42 in New York, 12 in New Jersey, and a dozen more elsewhere along the East coast.

Sandy made landfall about 8 p.m. October 29 near Atlantic City N.J. with winds of 80 mph. A full moon produced tides 20% higher than normal, amplifying the storm surge; the famed boardwalk was torn apart.

When Sandy reached New York City, seawater surged over lower Manhattan's sea walls into low-lying streets; inundating tunnels, subways and the electrical system that powers Wall Street. The surge topped 14 feet, surpassing the record set by hurricane Donna in 1960. Winds extended out 175 miles from its center.

Rising Seas

Less than one year later, September 9, 2013, the National Geographic featured global warming with the ominous headline **RISING SEAS** boldly on its cover. The cover displayed the Statue of Liberty submerged in some 50 feet of Hudson Bay water. The featured article reported this frightening future:

> **"As the world warms it may see more**
> **storms like Sandy; it will certainly see**
> **higher seas; a profoundly altered planet**
> **is what our fossil-fuel-driven civilization**
> **is creating."**

New York and Miami, two prominent east coast cities were the obvious focus of the flooding threat even though ocean waters flow around the planet. Presumably the source of flood water is the oceans; as temperatures warm the seas, the water expands.

This is a depressing prognosis indeed; millions upon millions of people forced to migrate inland to higher elevations.

Catastrophic Shortages

The notion of humans causing earth to warm and polar ice caps to melt is scary. Earth will heat up as we continue burning fossil fuels and exhaust more and more CO_2 into the atmosphere. As polar caps melt, massive amounts of water will flow into the oceans.

In 2004 several prominent executives issued this dire threat: "By **2020** catastrophic shortages of water and energy will become increasingly harder to overcome, plunging the planet into war . . ." Shortages of water, they say?

Formula for Disaster

A mathematic formula was constructed showing global temperatures rising proportional to airborne CO_2. Accordingly as CO_2 increases, earth's temperature rises.

Apparently increasing clouds and precipitation have no mitigating impact on relentless warming. Certainty (they say) is: CO_2 produces warming; warming melts polar ice; water from the ice caps raises the oceans, which then flood our cities. Warming is an inherent evil. No longer need one say: "We must stop warming because Miami (for instance) will disappear beneath the seas." Dire consequences are given.

Ocean Depths

Already, the alarmists say, oceans rose ½ inch from 1997 to 2010. The average depth was about 2.3 miles; this ½ inch represents a 0.00034 percent increase!

It is difficult to grasp how one can measure a ½ inch change in depth of oceans covering 90% of the globe; where sea elevations naturally vary from equator to the poles by 5 to 10 feet; where tides continually flow around the earth.

Robert Hotz, Professor, University of Washington, reported in the Wall Street Journal that arctic ice had been declining since 1970's. Yet seas did not rise! Then in late 2013 the volume of arctic ice was well above average. Yet seas did not decline! Where, we must wonder, is the science supporting the claim of world-wide flooding from global warming?

Consequences - Curtailing CO_2

Warmers are quick to tell us about the dire consequences of global warming - how polar ice caps will melt and flood the earth.

What about the flip side? What are the consequences of denying the world this ubiquitous source of energy. The GDP is a common measure of economic success and well-being. Here is the world-wide GDP per capita record for the last 50 years during which carbon energy consumption accelerated; mankind reaped enormous economic benefits of fossil fuels.

FIGURE 2: Carbon Economics

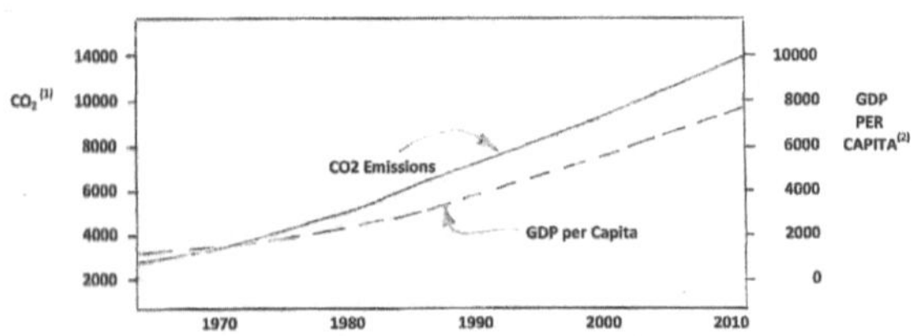

Notes to Figure 2

1. Carbon dioxide emissions are in millions of metric tons.
2. The world GDP is in 2010 dollars.
3. Sources of data: EPA and World Bank.

The world's Gross Domestic Product over the past 50 years grew by a factor of four from $2000 per capita to nearly $8000. Concurrently carbon dioxide emissions increased nearly in lock step, rising from 2000 to 10,000 million metric tons of CO_2; in doing so contributed immensely to the world's economic well being over the past century or more.

There are two critical questions we should ask at this point:

What price must we pay to forego carbon-based energy?

What will the world's people gain from this immense sacrifice?

We have yet to learn the answers to these critical questions.

V

BELIEVERS AND PROMOTERS

The weight of public information, news papers and TV, supporting the carbon-warming theory is overwhelming and nearly unchallenged. A search for organizations supporting warming found 350 not-for-profit organizations have adopted the carbon-warming theory and are actively promoting steps to curtail CO_2.

3,800 Gigatonnes Melted

NASA reported the continent of Greenland lost ice sheet volume in the amount of 3,800 gigatonnes over a 14-year period from 2002 to 2016.

Why did NASA not connect the dots from this report to world-wide flooding? I suspect they intended us to think that as Greenland's ice continues melting the oceans will rise; Manhattan will flood; other coastal cities will submerge under the seas; but they dare not say so.

Non-Event

What would happen if NASA is correct and these gigatonnes of ice melt actually flowed into the world oceans? Here's what they did not tells us: 3,800 gigatonnes of ice translates into a tiny fraction of an inch in ocean depth; that is 0.00000000046 inches. What NASA should have said is: Greenland's ice melt over the past 14 years had no measurable impact on ocean depths.

Nevertheless, believers still embrace three connected notions: planet earth is warming; warming is the consequence of increasing airborne CO_2; global temperatures increase proportionally to CO_2 in the atmosphere. All of this, they say, is settled science!

Earthly Non Compliance

Significant deviations from the formulated warming are evident in records over the last century. These deviations remain unexplained even though they are quite large relative to the fractional degrees of warming cited.

Climate modelers do not explain why global temperatures vary erratically while atmospheric CO_2 rises in small steady increments.

Furthermore, they offer no explanation as to the causes of ancient ice ages and subsequent warming; certainly these changes were not anthropogenic.

**Planet earth seems disinclined to
follow the warming play book.**

Shape of the Earth

Some time ago a headline in the Journal of Climate website caught my attention: "Rising ground in West Antarctica under melting Amundsen Sea Embayment of 4.1 centimeters per year".

Earth changes shape over centuries, but it does not grow; if it bulges in West Antarctic, it depresses elsewhere.

A recent volcanic eruption in Hawaii raised the question of lava flow displacing ocean water (thus raising the sea level); this too is a mass relocation. Earth temperatures shift around; lava brings heat to the surface; yet there is no increase in earth's mass. Earth maintains a nearly constant volume. Yes, temperature changes cause minimal expansion or contraction; otherwise topographic moves just push the shape around.

Managing the Threat

Dedicated scientists insist carbon is the devil even though the evidence is tenuous. We hardly know what to think.

It is common to equivocate. In 2015 Gina McCarty, Obama's EPA administrator, commenting on a temperature rise of 1/100th of a degree Celsius and knowing that this miniscule rise would get very little notice, said success should be measured in terms of U. S. leadership toward CO_2 abatement.

The International Panel on Climate Control (IPCC) reported thermal expansion over a recent 20 year period caused the ocean to rise one-half inch. (They did not mention that the average depth is about 2.3 miles.)

How could anyone measure a ½ inch change of depth over oceans covering 90% of the globe; oceans whose currents cause sur.face elevations to vary everywhere; whose surface elevation from the north and south poles to the equator varies by some 20 feet (240 inches) due to earth's rotation and the sun's gravity pull. Irrespective of this tiny ocean rise, we continue to be hounded by claims of world flooding.

Climate warming proponents insist that, no matter how tiny the warming or how miniscule the ocean rise, we must reduce CO_2 emissions. Holman Jenkins in the Wall Street Journal wrote: "This is akin to researchers claiming a new drug a success because it is detectable in the bloodstream!"

Managing the Facts

Facts be damned; the narrative is the thing:

"If the facts do not fit the narrative (of carbon-driven global warming), we must manage the facts."

This sounds evil; yet in 2009 at the University of East Anglia (Australia), a climate research unit reportedly was searching for a way to hide a temperature **decline**!

The Wall Street Journal, reported that, in a 2015 study by the National Oceanic and Atmospheric Administration (NOAA), temperature readings from certain ocean buoys had to be adjusted to match shipboard measurements to get accurate readings. Incidentally this adjustment overcame what would have shown as a pause in global warming!

Settled Science?

We are told by experts holding advanced degrees that climate science is settled. This is a hoax and an obvious one because science is never really settled. Centuries ago philosophers (philosophy being the nearest thing to science at the time) were certain that earth was flat . . . until it became apparent that it was round . . . they then conceded: the sun traveled around earth, arising in the east every morning and sinking in the west every evening! Over time that theory also failed as enlightened observers realized that the sun did not rotate around earth.

VI

ECONOMY GURUS

The climate mantra is: we must be weaned off carbon-based fuels else we are doomed. They promise we will not be hurt when we comply.

"The majority of American families will benefit financially by receiving more in carbon dividends than they will pay in increased energy prices."

This is trickle up economics; the costs are transferred upward to millionaires and evil corporations; for the rest of us carbon abatement is a free ride!

"Harmless" Carbon Pill

A statement was issued by 48 prominent economists titled: "Economists' Statement on Carbon Dividends". They recommend a carbon tax to reduce dependence on fossil fuels. This carbon tax would increase yearly to meet emission goals; we will be weaned from fossil fuels.

These economy gurus give us no hint as to how we will replace carbon-based fuels with cost-effective alternatives. They simply say: while consumers pay more for energy, they get dividends from the government to make them whole. Quite painless – like free lunches every day. Here the less carbon we burn, the greater our "carbon dividend".

We may pay more for fuel; but we get it back via government dividends. "All the revenue should be returned directly to citizens through equal rebates." Yea, economically we all come out even: banning carbon fuels economically is a break-even deal; while the average wage earner will get more in carbon dividends than he pays in higher energy prices.

Utopian economists offer us this win-win deal. Meanwhile corporations will not swallow this carbon pill; they cannot yet survive. They will do what they must – increase prices.

As consumers pay higher fuel costs; they may, or may not, be reimbursed by government. Meanwhile businesses raise prices to offset higher energy costs; and of course consumers pay more for their products.

Presumably most American families benefit financially by receiving more in carbon dividends than they pay in increased energy prices; the huge costs trickle up somehow to the nation's millionaires.

VII

BANDWAGON

A decade ago we were told climate differed from weather. Now every violent storm is a climate event. Every extreme – storm or even a California wild fire – is attributed to carbon emissions.

There were two pertinent weather articles in the local newspaper. One observed how much the world depends on coal. It was gratuitous; there was no recent climate or weather event reported.

In the second, the reporter casually equated recent stormy weather events to climate change; never mind that planet earth has had violent storms long before we found coal veins in western Pennsylvania.

Another Harvey

September 2017 a Wall Street Journal article titled "Insuring our coasts against the next Harvey" reported the flood damage Harvey caused Houston, Texas. The reporter was compelled to link this event to warming.

Climate change was responsible for Houston's disaster, he implied. Then he observed that 16% of the world's population will soon live in large coastal cities vulnerable to rising seas.

Oddly, Houston's elevation is 40 feet above sea level; at no risk from rising seas.

Settling Science by Attribution

Over the past 10 years or so climate "science" morphed into a political cult: the science is settled; we must curtail carbon emissions; government must change our behavior.

Any unusual weather event is routinely attributed to carbon emissions. There is a massive effort and billions of dollars supporting and promoting this belief system.

Climate Wagon Assumptions

There are more than 350 non-profit organizations on the internet calling for a draconian reduction in fossil fuel consumption. For them, carbon-induced global warming is a given; accepted without question. None are scientific; all are advocacy driven. They accept the tenet that carbon-induced warming is settled science.

Their climate dogma assumes the sun's impact on earth is benign; that the effect of the sun remains constant over the centuries; that earth's climate swings are driven by atmospheric CO_2.

There are three suspect assumptions here. First, 40% of CO_2 emissions will be retained in the atmosphere. Second, atmospheric CO_2 retention is cumulative and linear. Third, global temperatures will rise in direct proportion to increasing airborne CO_2. All of these assumptions are hypothetical!

Beyond these suspects, Believers do not recognize earth's natural responses to warming – especially increasing cloud formation and precipitation. Oddly, these effects are claimed to be part of the warming dogma.

Incontrovertible Edict

The evidence is incontrovertible says the American Physical Society:

> **"Global warming is occurring. If no mitigating actions are taken, significant disruptions in the earth's physical and ecological systems, social systems, security and human health are likely to occur. We must reduce greenhouse gasses now."**

Political Wisdom

Irrespective of the uncertainties about warming, we are told by democrat/socialist presidential aspirants that climate Armageddon is just a decade away.

According to Alexandria Ocasio-Cortez, we have a mere decade until dooms day:

> **"The world is going to end in twelve years**
> **if we don't address climate change."**

This is a bit dramatic. She does not explain what catastrophe is on the way; **IT** (whatever **IT** may be) will happen in the year 2030, give or take two.

Here we are: environmental Armageddon nearly upon us; and when it arrives, planet earth will have irreversibly warmed; millions will race to the hills as oceans rise and flood coastal cities.

Crimes of Denial

Senator Whitehouse suggested using the RICO law (which targets organized crime) against people who questioned the carbon induced global warming theory. It was reported that the matter was referred to the FBI's criminal investigation division. In time Senator Whitehouse "graciously" stopped trying to shut down scientific debate through criminal actions; instead he "generously" decided civil prosecutions of climate dissenters would be sufficient.

Penn State professor Michael Mann is suing the National Review because it published a 270-word blog criticizing Mr.

Mann for what they termed his "fraudulent" hockey stick graph.

Other "Expert" Prescriptions

The Wall Street Journal published an Op Ed titled "Capitalism Will Solve the Climate Problem" by Fred Krupp, President of the Environmental Defense Fund (WSJ 7/23/18).

This Op Ed is long on hyperbole and short on science. Krupp wrote: "Atmospheric scientists predicted increased frequency of extreme-heat events; and they were right, too." Except that extreme events in the last 100 years have occurred randomly.

Mr. Krupp thinks storms weren't very bad 30 years ago. He wrote: "Storms are more intense than they were 30 years ago, due to warmer oceans and other climate-related factors". Mr. Krupp adds: ""Best available research confirms human-driven climate change." (30 years ago earth was recovering from a cold spell.)

The correlation between global temperatures and CO_2 is quite poor; moreover unexplained global temperature variations are larger than variations explained by increasing CO_2. Where, we must ask, is the research Mr. Krupp refers to?

Hedge Your Bet

Hedging is a device to lower investment risk. It is an appropriate investment tactic in the face of uncertainty.

When the Greenland ice sheet melts, oceans will rise 25 feet. Just imagine what that will do to our cities? Bye-bye New York City; and much of Florida – mostly just a few feet above sea level! Already the seas have risen ½ inches; before that the average ocean depth was 2.3 miles!

Perhaps you should hedge your bet - buy a canoe before they're sold out, or before you have no gasoline to drive to the marine store, whichever comes first.

Science by Survey

A large number of climate scientists believe climate change, that is warming, is anthropogenic (caused by humans). They assert that 97% of their associates also believe climate change is man-made and urgent.

This claim was derived from a survey of 79 respondents who listed climate science as an area of their expertise. Yes, we knew the earth was flat centuries ago by polling the experts, who then were philosophers.

VIII

JUST THE FACTS

Science relies on verifiable facts. Hypotheses are useful, but they need proven before accepted as science. Climate science is far from settled.

There is uncertainty about global temperatures; about the relationship between CO_2 and global temperatures; and indeed about the validity of global temperature claims. Adding to these uncertainties, there seems to be a lot of manipulation behind the published data.

Temperature Tinkering

It has been reported that government temperature data for 1880 to 2010 has been tinkered with 16 times. Especially disturbing: reported earth temperature variations from place to place, season to season, and year to year are far larger than those attributed to the carbon effect.

Over the last 17 years temperatures leveled out while we continued to consume carbon-based fuels! Yet they insist the science is settled!

CO_2 Airborne Retention Rate

After a century of burning fossil fuels, the atmosphere now contains 4 parts of CO_2 per 10,000. Moreover, it appears that the ratio of CO_2 additions compared to the net retention **is declining**.

Celestial Influence

Warming "science" presumes airborne CO_2 is the sole driver of climate; neither the sun nor other solar factor matters much. Yet here are five other events that drive climate:

- Earth's surface crust keeps changing slowly.
- Continents move, changing ocean currents.
- Earth's orbit adjusts to outer universe changes.
- Volcanoes erupt.
- Sun's energy output varies.

The sun's energy, hence its brightness, varies on all timescales on which it has been observed, and there is increasing evidence that this has an influence on climate. The main drivers of solar variability are thought to be magnetic features on the surface of the sun. [1]

Cosmic Rays

"The earth is a traveler. It circles the black hole at the galaxy's core every 226 million years, taking its tiny flock of planets with it. Every 143 million years we pass through a spiral arm of the galaxy, an arm that tosses tsunamis of cosmic rays our way. These cosmic rays produce massive climate change." [2]

Cooling Interlude

From early in the industrial revolution, airborne CO_2 and global temperatures mostly increased. Recently, though, temperatures took a turn for the worse (cooling) while emissions continued unabated.

Some suggest the warming hiatus was due to an anomaly out in the Pacific Ocean where missing solar heat accumulated but was not recorded. Others claim cooler ocean waters lowered the global temperature! Where is the settled science when we need it?

---

[1] See "Solar Irradiance Variability and Climate" in Astronomy and Astrophysics 6/26/2013.

[2] Excerpt from "Climate Change is Nature's Way" by Howard Bloom, founder Space Development Steering Committee.

A Failing Grade

The claim of CO_2-driven global warming does not withstand a basic test: recorded temperatures differ significantly from theoretical expectations. Why? Just maybe there are other factors in the solar system that impact on climate!

Of course there really are other factors that influence out climate; including sun spots, earth wobble, solar system changes, and earth's natural defenses.

Bygone Ages

Earth has gone through massive temperature changes over the ages. According to Climate4you, over the past 400,000 years global temperatures exceeded current levels five times. Yes, temperatures periodically rose above current levels without our help. "Climate science" does not account for them, or even try.

Wobble

Wobble refers to earth's axis. As the axis tilts it is said to wobble. [3]There are multiple theories about this. One is wobble is caused by melting ice caps – which change earth's weight distribution. Another is the opposite notion - wobble causes ice caps to melt.

The most likely explanation is that changes in earth's weight distribution causes wobble; such as movements of

---

[3] See Appendix B: Precession and Wobbles)

water and ice, or mass movements within earth's molten core.

Additionally natural forces in the solar system play a much larger role than recognized. Judith Curry, professor of atmospheric sciences, Georgia Institute of Technology, says there is too much uncertainty around climate models; and that it is unlikely that humans have as much influence on climate as natural forces.

Professor Curry believes the climate models that predict catastrophic warming are not valid. On her web site she writes:

> **"We need to go back to basics to get the fundamental interactions between the ocean and atmosphere correct, because this is what driving the whole thing. In climate modeling all the eggs were put into one basket, and we've gotten as far as we're going to get along that particular path. We need to start over with a new path for climate modeling."**

Professor Curry already has taken this thought about a new path one step forward. In testimony before the House Committee on Government Reform (July 2006), she presented a chart showing the number of storms in the North Atlantic compared to the sea surface temperatures. Not surprising, there was a high correlation between the two from 1850 to 2010. [4]

---

[4] Global Warming and Hurricanes, 2006

It is tempting to claim these storms are evidence of CO_2-induced global warming. Alternatively, this is exactly what we should expect of earth.

**Storms increase as planet earth reacts;
mitigating any warming trend.**

Of course! Increasing storms is earth's response to warming.

IX

GREENLAND SCAM

We think of Greenland as a small continent near the North Pole. Wikipedia defines it as the world's largest non-continental island - 836,000 square miles.

Recently Greenland has become the focus of climate doomsayers because (supposedly) it has an ice cap sufficient to flood the world if it should melt.

Several years ago Robert Hotz reported in the WSJ article "Arctic Ice Is Able To Rebuild, Study Says" that a steady decline in the extent of Arctic sea ice since the late 1970's has been taken as a barometer of longer-term warming trends in the Northern hemisphere.

Hotz wrote that in late 2013 the volume of sea ice was well above average after an unusually cool summer. But sea levels did not decline as the volume of ice grew.

The primary reason for the disconnect between Greenland ice and world ocean levels is the large inland sea; it is relevant and must be accounted for.

This Greenland inland sea is a vast body of a frozen sea who's waters are partly below and partly above sea level. Recently a mega channel running nearly the length of Greenland through the sea was discovered. This frozen sea ice cannot cause flooding; instead it tends to do the reverse: upon melting it's volume contracts below sea level, causing the sea level to decline, not rise.

Ocean Expansion

When ocean water warms or cools, its volume expands or contracts a bit; ocean level changes accordingly. Mostly these are regional changes that produce ocean currents flowing to equalize water pressures around the world.

Warming begins at the surface and penetrates downward to the thermocline, some 3000 feet below sea level.

Thermal expansion during the most intense period of CO_2 emissions, 1997 to 2010, is said to have caused oceans to rise approximately ½ inch. For perspective that ½ inch is 0.00034 percent increase in ocean depth.

Oceans cover 90% of the globe; its spinning motion causes ocean surface elevations to vary from poles to the equator. Entire continents shift ground over the centuries, adding confusion to ocean depths.

Hedging the Threat

Former Secretary of State George Shultz wrote: "The risks associated with warming are so severe that they should be hedged." How about the risk of another ice age? Which risk should we hedge against – freezing or warming? An ice age would do far greater damage; in which case **we don't dare abandon fossil fuels.**

Flooding Farce

The threat of the Greenland ice sheet melting and flooding the world is a farce; without it there is no meaningful warming risk. Here we have a bit of Wikipedia weighing in on Greenland's geography:

> **"The weight of the ice sheet has depressed the central land area to form a basin lying more than 300 meters (984 feet) below sea level (the inland sea), while elevations rise steeply near the coast."**

What happens when this ice sheet melts? As ice begins melting from the top, the melt flows toward the seas. As warming penetrates the inland sea, low-lying ice melts and contracts; then there is a back flow to refill the void.

This process is critical to world sea levels. Water from melting ice lying above the Greenland Sea fills the void created by contraction of below-sea-level ice melt. Only the remaining overflow, if any, runs to the oceans.

The Greenland overflow residual going into the oceans (if the ice cap were to melt completely) could raise the seas six inches, possibly less. (Alarmists claim the oceans would rise 25 feet.)

Several years ago William Happer, Atomic Physicist and Professor at Princeton University, wrote this about the claim that a Greenland meltdown would cause world flooding:

> **"Of course there is not a chance that all the Greenland ice will melt. The ice did not melt in the previous, Eemian interglacial, about 125,000 years ago, which was much warmer than our current one. Greenland's location next to the gulf stream at high latitudes makes it hard to avoid massive snow buildup."**

"Not a chance" he said. Meanwhile, there is no other meaningful climate threat to the human race in sight. Yes, the Greenland threat really is a scam.

REAL WORLD

The impact of clouds on Earth's climate varies at different elevations in the atmosphere. Some block the sun's rays, while others produce a greenhouse effect, preventing heat from escaping earth. According to both NASA and the National Science Foundation, on balance, clouds produce a cooling effect.

Science Evolution

What we believe as scientific truth evolves as our understanding of the world and the solar system advances. Recall several centuries ago people believed the earth was flat; and it might have stayed flat if Columbus hadn't sailed around the world.

Lost Generation

Diverted by claims that climate science is settled, we have lost decades not inquiring deeply into the dynamics of earth's climate within the solar system. Earth science cannot do justice to this topic, climate, without a broader perspective. Dr. Judith Curry wrote that we simply do not know enough about climate:

> **"We've ceded all that to climate models, and the climate models are nowhere good enough. Climate models were designed to test sensitivity to CO_2. They don't even do a very good job at that. All the issues related to the sun/climate connections, decadal to millennial scale, circulation and oscillation in the ocean and the deep carbon cycle in the oceans. Some of these things we fundamentally don't know enough about."** [5]

---

[5] Dr. Judith Curry in the E & E News, Jan 4, 2017

Wild Card

As global temperature inches upward, earth reacts to bring itself back into equilibrium. It does so according to this five-step process:

1. Earth warms
2. Surface waters evaporate
3. More clouds form
4. Participation (rain, sleet, snow) increases.
5. Earth cools

Earth adjusts to the warming effect of CO_2: this is a natural response. Here's how Physicist Dr. Clive Best describes the process:

> **"The natural cyclic change in global cover has a greater impact on global temperatures than CO_2. The gradual reduction in cloud cover explains over 50% of global warming observed during the 80's and 90's, and the hiatus in warming since 1998 coincides with a stabilization of cloud forcing."**

Apparently the National Science Foundation agrees more or less with this comment: "Clouds are the wild card of climate change." Even more telling about clouds is the statement by NASA's Earth Observatory:

> **Just a 5% increase in cloud reflectivity could compensate for the entire increase**

in greenhouse gases from the modern industrial era.

In other words, it is quite easy for earth to neutralize the carbon - warming effect.

Sounding the Atmosphere

Launched in 2001, SABER (Sounding of the Atmosphere using Broadband Emission Radiometry) was the first comprehensive attempt at measuring the upper atmosphere. According to James Russel, Hampton University and SABER's principal investigator, carbon dioxide and nitric oxide are natural thermostats.

When the upper atmosphere heats up, these molecules increase their resistance.

As CO_2 rises into the thermosphere it has a cooling effect by providing a heat shield.

Wow! CO_2 cooling the earth! That's a novel idea.

What Warming?

In recent years temperature records do not support the warming theory. Here we have a compilation showing global temperature changes compared to carbon dioxide in five year increments since 1980. This tabulation was derived from NOAA data.

FIGURE 3: Temperature vs. CO_2 - 1980 to 2015

PERIOD	$+CO_2$	TEMP GAIN	TEMP/CO_2
1980-1985	4	0	0.000^0
1985-1990 8	+0.2	0.025^0	
1990-1995	6	0	0.000^0
1995-2000	9	+0.2	0.022^0
2000-2005	8	+0.1	0.011^0
2005-2010	11	-0.1	-0.009^0
2010-2015	9	+0.3	0.033^0

CO_2 is atmospheric carbon dioxide in parts per million.

The global warming threat derives from the claim that CO_2 is **the** cause; yet here we see the correlation between them is almost nonexistent. Even in periods where the temperature increased, variations (.01 to .03 degrees centigrade) are beyond incidental explanation.

Warmers say non-conforming periods are natural events that influence global temperatures. However these anomalies overwhelm the rules of climate change.

Cloud Cooling

There are cloud formations at various elevations in the atmosphere. Some block sun's rays while others produce a greenhouse effect. According to the National Science Foundation, on balance clouds cool the earth.

"Clouds cover 67% of the earth at all times and a 1% variance in cloud

cover would wipe out the entire 0.80 C warming associated with CO_2." [6]

Astronomy

"Earth is a traveler; its angle as it sweeps around the sun produces massive weather changes." [7]

The solar system drives earth's climate. Physicist Dr. Clive Best confirms this:

> **"It really is the sun that causes global warming not CO_2 at all. All that increasing CO_2 does is adjust the radiative profile with altitude."**

Perhaps shocking to many, here we have crux of the issue. Carbon may cause some redistribution; but earth's climate balance is driven by the sun.

> **"The gradual reduction in net cloud cover explains over 50% of global atmosphere warming observed during the 80s and 90s; and the hiatus in warming since 1998 coincides with a stabilization of cloud forcing."**

As early as 2003 a NASA scientist admitted that solar radiation is the dominant, direct energy input into the

---

[6] "A Cool Experience" by John S. Thomas

[7] "The Real Inconvenient Truth: It's Warming: but it's Not CO_2," by M. J. Sangster, PhD.

terrestrial ecosystem. Variations in sun's heat rays, and the effects of the vast universe impact on earth's climate. Of course the sun provides a natural influence on the earth's atmosphere.

Many Astrophysicists recognize there are other factors driving our climate. For instance, the Annual Review of Astronomy and Astrophysics, June 2010 wrote:

> **It is virtually impossible to assign the minimal global warming of the past half century to variations in solar irradiance alone.**

Wobbling

Earth has a tendency to wobble; its axis osculates in relation to the sun, changing hemispheric exposures. Recordings that favor the Northern hemisphere do not produce global averages.

West Antarctica Wonder

The Journal of Climate web site reports: "Rising ground in West Antarctica under melting Amundsen Sea Embayment of 4.1 cm/yr."

This is climate static! Earth's mass is constant; water evaporates, condenses and returns to ground. When West Antarctic land rises, it merely pushes water around; earth's mass stays constant.

Gang of Three hundred and Fifty

There are 350 non-profit "ban CO_2," advocacy organizations. They have huge endowments that crowd out cautionary voices. They say risks are overwhelming. Just 10 years ago the warming risk was specified as: earth warms; seas rise: continents flood. Dire consequences are no longer specified; they are givens.

Green New Deal

The "Green New Deal" was introduced in Congress by Representative Alexandria Ocasio-Cortez of New York and Senator J. Markey of Massachusetts. It lays out a grand plan for the federal government to curtail fossil fuels.

According to the Competitive Enterprise Institute, the Green New Deal would cost some $8 to $12 trillion; that is more than $50,000 per household. Of course corporations will pay the tab! Wrong! They will do what they must - increase prices. The economics are elementary:

- Consumers pay higher fuel costs.
- Consumers get reimbursed by government.
- Businesses pay more taxes.
- Consumers pay more for goods and services.

Carbon abolitionists demand we tax carbon-based fuels out of existence; the government can compensate us through carbon dividends. We will pay more for energy but get it back in carbon dividends. Three cheers for voodoo economics!

The World at Risk

People world over have been gaining economically since the industrial revolution. Average wealth, as measured by GDP per capita, increased from approximately $8,000 per capita in 1900 to $55,000 last year. This is an incredible gain in prosperity; and it has paralleled the increase in consumption of carbon-based fuels and consequently the increasing CO_2 in the world's atmosphere.

The world's rapidly expanding economy is at grave risk from the intentions of the "Green New Deal" and like-minded "warmers" to curtail CO_2 who have no economic alternative to offer.

Good News Abounds

A problem for the global warming threat is the welfare of the entire world keeps getting better. Look at the record since 1950 as reported by the Competitive Enterprise Institute:

- Life expectancy increased 23 years
- Malaria deaths are down 62%
- Corn yields are up 88% since 1980
- Global poverty is sharply down

Simple Truths

While we meditate on the prospects of global warming, or listen to political orators lecture us about it, we should be mindful of these simple truths:

> **After more than a century burning fossil fuels non-stop, our atmosphere contains just 4 parts of CO_2 per 10,000.**
>
> **An amount equal to two-thirds of CO_2 emissions gets "rinsed" out of the atmosphere every year.**
>
> **The atmosphere is moving toward a saturation point; every year it retains a lesser portion of CO_2 emissions.**
>
> **Recent non-warming temperatures contradict the CO_2-driven warming formula.**

What Fills the Void?

Planet Earth has a volume of about $1.097\text{x}10^{21}$ cubic meters of solids, molten ores, and water. This volume does not change much from century to century. So then how do we get a massive amount of water rising up and flooding the world's continents? Where does all of this water come from? Melting polar ice caps? (We must keep reminding ourselves that melting ice contracts in volume; melting ice below sea level causes sea levels to contract, not rise.)

XI

A SIMPLE QUESTION

Long ago there were ice ages - ancient events taking place before mankind. That the earth passed through periods of extreme cold should make us wonder about the in-between periods: the warming that followed each ice age. What caused that warming?

Warmers cannot answer that simple question (nor other critical questions); their claim of warming from carbon dioxide remains hypothetical.

Scientific principles are not matters of convenience; to be turned on and off to accommodate current fashions like the flat-earth centuries ago. Nor is it a matter of majority support as polling produces opinions, not science.

One of the most active environmentalists over the last 40 years was Michael Shellenberger, founder of "Environmental Progress". Recently he apologized for the climate scare he helped along. In "Apocalypse Never" he exposes the motivations of the environmental groups and their doomsday pronouncements.

If We Could Do That

If we could change earth's climate balance by curtailing CO_2, then why not tweak global climate to an optimal temperature for mankind's greatest comfort and collective wealth. Yes, if we could do that then why reject the blessings of CO_2 in favor of a harsher life?

Reality, while inconvenient to those invested in the CO_2 warming dogma, is that earth's eco-system is self-correcting. Warm temperatures cause water to evaporate and rise into the sky; clouds form and eventually become storms returning water and cooling the planet.

Further, clouds provide cover and protection from strong sun rays. The cloud process accelerates as needed as earth reacts to retain its climate equilibrium.

There is no compelling scientific reason for drastic action to de-carbonize the world; and art lovers have no need to fear the Statue of Liberty will get her feet wet from rising waters.

AFTERWORD

The main threat of global warming, we are told, is melting polar ice caps; resulting in rising seas and global flooding.

In recent years global warming morphed into a political mantra. Early on in 2006 it was Al Gore's "An Inconvenient Truth" forecasting doomsday some 20 years out. Now we have presidential candidates promising us a "Green New Deal".

This "Green New Deal" proposes to ameliorate the risk of catastrophic warming coming upon us over the next 10 years. The cost is enormous; but, we will get a free ride as corporate America and its wealthy owners foot the bill.

We are not so naïve not to notice the lack of substance behind this Armageddon threat. Our imperative is to arm ourselves with knowledge of the risks and enormous costs of abandoning carbon-based energy; else the financial consequences will be catastrophic.

APPENDIX A
GREENLAND MELTDOWN

As an ice cube floats in a glass of water or tea, part of the cube shows above the surface. Yet when it melts, the water level does not rise! Of course - ice is lighter than water. (Specific gravity of ice is about 92 %.) When it melts, it contracts.

The same thing happens when floating ice bergs melt. The level of the ocean does not change. Melting ice causes the sea to rise **only** when the ice is grounded on land above sea level, hence cannot float.

A more complex condition arises when the ice sheet rests on solid ground below sea-level (such as an inland sea). This ice cannot float as its mass above sea level weighs it down. Here the ice above sea level will flow to the ocean as it melts; but in a complete meltdown, the water will backflow into the inland sea as the ice further melts and contracts.

When floating ice melts, it contracts and the water volume created is equal to the volume of ice that had been submerged below sea level; there is no increase in water level.

Earth's water volume is essentially constant, hence oceans rise only when ice masses above sea level grounded on land melt. A portion, but not all, of the Greenland ice sheet is so grounded.

However, Greenland has a vast frozen inland sea covering about 1/3 of the continent. Generally the outer perimeter of this sea is rising land and mountains, then falling to the ocean.

Some years ago, the National Geographic projected 23.5 ft ocean rise if the Greenland ice sheet were to melt. This forecast assumed all of the Greenland ice-melt would flow to the ocean. Reality would be quite different. The density of the ice sheet varies from 10% (of water) at the very top (pure dry snowfall) to something approaching 90% in the lower depths (ice with gas inclusions).

Were the Greenland ice sheet to melt, the large frozen inland sea would act as a reservoir: its ice contraction creating a void for ice lying above-sea-level.

Another error is not allowing for an increased ocean surface as it rises and spreads onto sea-side land. As the surface area expands, so does it take more volume increase for each foot of increased depth. This oversight would be significant with a rise of 20 feet, but little more than a footnote were the oceans to rise 5 feet or less.

APPENDIX 3
PRECESSION AND WOBBLE

The earth rotates around its axis. Nominally this axis is a line through the north and south poles. Over time the axis tilts - in slow motion. There is a repetitive cycle to tilting; it is called precession and it repeats every 26,000 years. What, you may fairly ask, does precession have to do with climate?

Precession affects the distribution of ocean water around the earth; as the axis changes; ocean water finds a new equilibrium with gravitational and centrifugal forces. The change in water distribution does not alter the to.tal volume of earth's water. However as the axis tilts a bit, waters rise in some regions, offset by water receding elsewhere. The impact of precession on ocean movement over a short geological period such as a century is quite small. But over multi-centuries, tilting of the earth axis can change ocean levels, some higher and some lower, regionally. For instance, when the angle of earth's axis verses the sun decreases, ocean waters flow toward the north and south poles; while mid-globe waters ebb a bit.

There are axis movements in addition to wobbles. Where there is a wobble, it is caused by significant weight redistributions somewhere within the earth - weight shifts as often evidenced by earthquakes or volcano eruptions.

It has been suggested that a large volume of water from melting ice flowing from one part of the globe to another could change the dynamics of the earth's rotation and cause axis wobble.

That idea is speculative as there has not been a sufficient volume of ice melting in the last few centuries to measurably change the dynamics of earth's rotation. It is far more likely that earth's ocean shifts are a consequence, not a cause, of wobble.

Wobble caused by an astronomical force change also could cause ocean movements. Such movements could cause flooding, but the result would be regional not global, as rising waters in some regions are countered by receding waters elsewhere.

APPENDIX C
REFERENCES AND SOURCES

PAGE TEXT REFERENCES

i   An Inconvenient Truth: Al Gore, former VP

5.   Global Temperatures: NOAA

6.   Lower Troposphere Temperatures: Climate4you

9.   Cato Institute: Patrick Michaels

10.   Cloud Cover: Clive Best, Physicist

13.   Atmospheric CO_2 History: NOAA

19.   Rising Seas: National Geographic 9/9/2013

20.   Artic Ice: Prof. Robert Hotz: U. of Washington

23.   Greenland Ice Melting: NASA

24.   Rising Ground: Journal of Climate

25.   Global Temperatures: Gina McCarty, EPA

26.   Climate Research: University of East Angela

26.   NOAA Report: Wall Street Journal 2015

27.   Carbon Dividends: 48 Economists

30. Hurricane Harvey: Wall Street Journal 2017

31. Warming: American Physical Society

32. Climate Dissenters: Senator Whitehouse

32. Legal action: Prof. Michael Mann, Penn State U.

33. Capitalism & Climate: WSJ 7/23/18: Fred Krupp

36. Solar Impact: Astronomy & Astrophysics 6/26/13

37. Climate Change is Nature's Way: Howard Bloom

39. Climate Models: Judith Curry, Professor

40. Artic Ice: Robert Hotz, Wall Street Journal

42. Climate Risk: George Shultz, Secretary of State

43. Greenland: William Happer, Professor, Princeton

46. Warming: Clive Best, Physicist

46. Atmosphere Behavior: James Russel, SABER

48. A Cool Experience: John S. Thomas

48. The Real Inconvenient Truth: J. Sangster, PhD

49. Review of Astronomy and Astrophysics, June 2013

53. Environmental Progress: Michael Shellenberger

ARTWORK SOURCES

Artwork, except Appendix D and the exhibit on page 20, was selected from the web site openclipart.org.

Artwork for Appendix D is from the book "So Mr. Mayor, You Want To Improve Productivity . . . ", written by yours truly and published by the National Commission on Productivity in 1974.

The graph "Carbon Economics", page 20, was drawn by the author using public data sources.

OTHER REFERENCES

Statement before Senate Environment Committee 2/25/14 by Patrick Moore, Ph.D., Greenpeace Founder.

Summary Climate Assessment: from Space & Science, by John Casey 2014.

Global Warming: The Best Schools interview with William Happer 5/23/2020.

Carbon Dioxide and Global Warming: CO2 Science 11/6/14.

APPENDIX D

THE AUTHOR

In the winter of 1968 New York City experienced a devastating snow blizzard; transportation was paralyzed, public schools closed, business slowed to a trickle.

The NYC Department of Sanitation is responsible to collect and dispose of trash and garbage. Unlike most cities, NYC uses its own collection trucks and municipal crews. The city owned 1800 trash collection trucks serving 1600 collection routes throughout five boroughs. These trucks doubled as snow plows by mounting plows on the front.

This snowstorm caught the City woefully unprepared. Sanitation was unable to clear snow-bound streets; transportation came to a halt; uncollected refuse piled up. I was a management consultant hired by the Mayor's Project Management unit to fix this problem; and to assure that it would not happen again.

The time to shuttle trucks back and forth to the central repair garage in Queens, and the wait time in the repair backlog were excessive; too many trucks were out of service every day and collection routes suffered. Worse, they were unable to plow the streets.

While the problem was complex, the key to maintaining collection schedules (and having plows available to clear the streets) was to decentralize repairs from the central garage in Queens to each of the other four boroughs. The new satellite repair shops reduced the turn-around times from days to hours; collection crews were able to complete schedules on time.

Improving government performance became recognized by Mayor Lindsay as a prime management responsibility; I was appointed Deputy Director of the Budget to oversee a city-wide productivity improvement program.

The Parks Department reorganized maintenance personnel into mobile crews, each servicing dozens of small parks dispersed throughout the city; doubling (or better) worker productivity.

A crime analysis in the police department (NYPD) found conventional work shifts were too rigid to cope with actual crime patterns. NYPD established a fourth platoon, increasing police coverage in the high crime hours of 6 pm to 2 am, and dramatically increasing apprehension rates.

Subsequently I was engaged by the National Commission on Productivity and Work Quality (whose Chairman was Nelson Rockefeller, Vice President of the United States) to advise local governments toward improving municipal productivity across the nation.

I authored of "So, Mr. Mayor, You Want to Improve Productivity . . . ". This handbook aimed to help local governments apply business management methods to improve performance.

"So Mr. Mayor . . ." was delivered to every local government chief executive in the nation. I devoted two years coaching executives from Boston to Honolulu to improve productivity; returning greater worth to the people for their tax dollars.

Beyond this public service, I am a management consultant; devoted to advising corporations domestic and world-wide as well as the United States Department of Defense.